Alfred's Kid's Guitar Course
Notespeller 1 & 2

Music Reading Activities that Make Learning Even Easier!

Ron Manus • L.C. Harnsberger

Alfred Music Publishing Co., Inc.
P.O. Box 10003
Van Nuys, CA 91410-0003
alfred.com

ISBN-10: 0-7390-1094-8
ISBN-13: 978-0-7390-1094-5

Contents

The Staff and Treble Clef

Guitar music is usually written on a five-line *staff*.
The lines are numbered from the bottom up.

5
4
3
2
1

At the beginning of each staff
is a *treble clef* that looks like this:

How to Draw the Treble Clef

Step 1:   Draw a circle under the staff and fill it in.

Step 2:   Draw a curved line (like the letter "u") that starts from the bottom of the circle
and touches the bottom of the first line of the staff.

Step 3:   Draw a line up from the first line to the fifth line.

Step 4:   Draw a loop above the second line of the staff.

Step 5:   Draw a long curving line that goes around the second line of the staff.

Now, draw six treble clefs below.

3

Bar Lines and Measures

Bar lines divide the staff into equal parts called *measures*. A *double bar line* is used at the end to show you the music is finished.

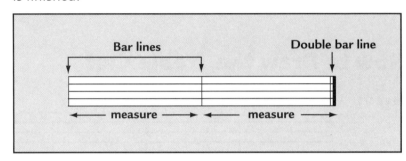

How to Draw Measures

Draw bar lines and a double bar line.

Draw the treble clef, bar lines, and double bar line to make four measures.

Make the same four measures again.

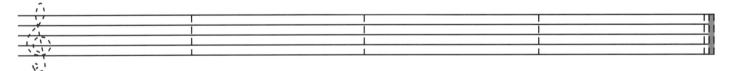

4

The 4/4 Time Signature

A *time signature* tells you how many beats are in a measure.
A 4/4 time signature means there are four equal beats in every measure.

How to Draw the 4/4 Time Signature

Step 1: Draw a number "4" sitting on top of the third line of the staff.

Step 2: Draw a second "4" below the first one, sitting on the bottom line.

Now, draw six 4/4 time signatures.

The Quarter-Note Slash

A slash with a stem is called a *quarter-note slash*.
Each quarter-note slash equals one beat.

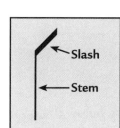

Slash

Stem

How to Draw the Quarter-Note Slash

Step 1: Create the slash by drawing a slanted line from the second staff line to the fourth staff line.

Step 2: Create the stem by drawing a line from the bottom of the slash to just below the staff.

Now, draw six quarter-note slashes.

5

Counting Time

Draw four quarter-note slashes in each measure.

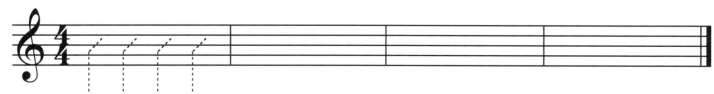

Write the counts for each measure below the quarter-note slashes.

Draw four measures including a treble clef, ¼ time signature, bar lines, a double bar line, and four quarter-note slashes in each measure. Then, write the counts below the measures.

The Three-String C Chord

Chord Diagrams

When reading a chord diagram, you will see exactly where to put your fingers. Each vertical line represents one of the six strings of the guitar: from left to right, 6 5 4 3 2 1. An **x** above a string means do not play it, and sometimes that string will also be shown as a dashed line. An **o** above a string means it is played open (not fingered). A circled number on a string shows you which finger to use and where to place it on that string.

Three-String C Chord

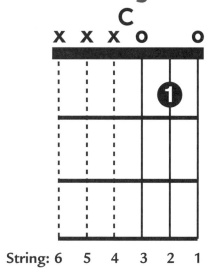

String: 6 5 4 3 2 1

Write the chord symbol "C" three times.

Draw the **x**'s, **o**'s, and fingering for the three-string C chords below.

C

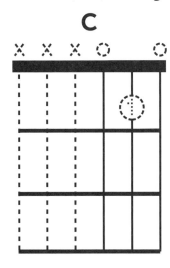

C

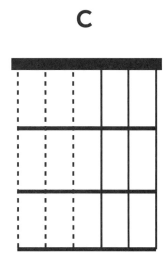

The Quarter Rest

Quarter Rest

The *quarter rest* means to be silent for one beat.

How to Draw the Quarter Rest

Step 1: Draw a short line slanting down from left to right.

Step 2: Draw a longer line slanting down from right to left starting at the bottom of the first line.

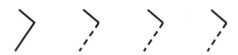

Step 3: Draw another short line slanting down from left to right starting at the bottom of the second line.

Step 4: Draw a curled line, almost like a letter "c," starting at the bottom of the third line.

Now, draw five quarter rests.

Counting Time

Fill in the missing beats with quarter rests.

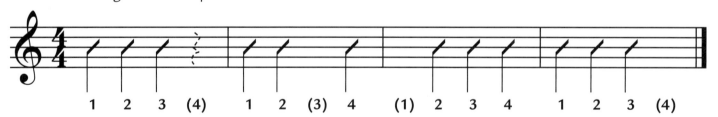

Write the counts below the staff. Put parentheses around the counts that are for rests.

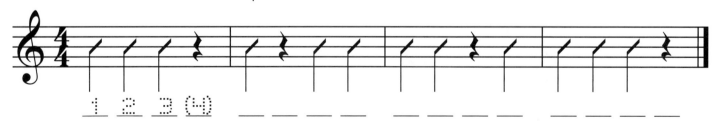

8

The Three-String G7 and G Chords

Three-String G⁷ Chord

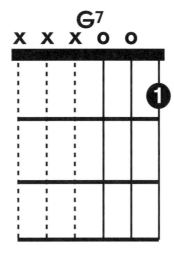

Write the chord symbol "G⁷" three times.

Three-String G Chord

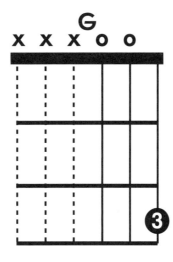

Write the chord symbol "G" three times.

Finish drawing the **x**'s, **o**'s, and fingering for the chords below.

G⁷

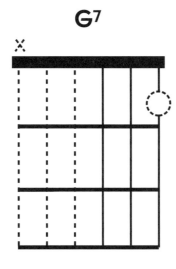

G

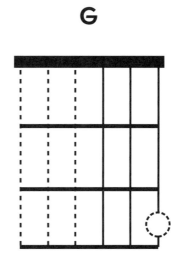

The Repeat Sign

When *double dots* are written on the inside of a double bar line, it makes a *repeat sign*. A repeat sign means to go back to the beginning and play the same music again.

How to Draw the Repeat Sign

Draw repeat signs by adding double dots to these double bar lines.

Draw a double bar line above each "Don't Repeat," and draw a repeat sign above each "Repeat."

Repeat   **Don't Repeat**   **Repeat**   **Repeat**   **Don't Repeat**

10

The Three-String D7 Chord

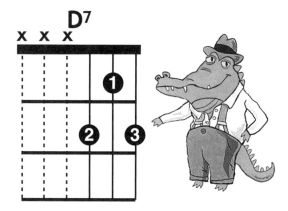

Write the chord symbol "D⁷" three times.

D^7

Draw the **x**'s and **o**'s for these chords.

D^7 G^7 G C

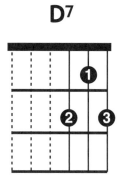 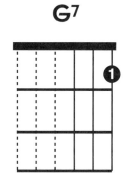 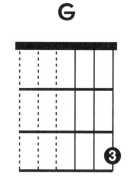 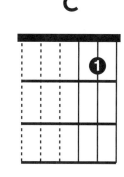

Let's Practice Writing Music

Finish creating four measures of music by tracing the treble clefs, time signature, bar lines, quarter-note slashes, quarter rests, repeat sign, and chord frames.

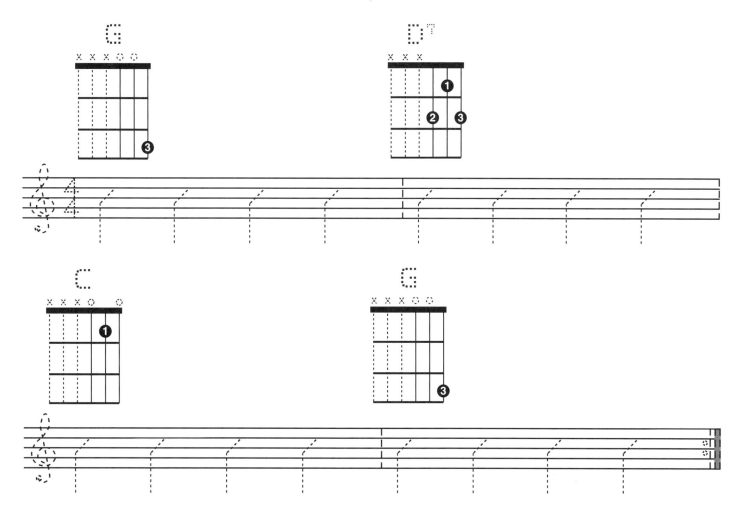

Write Your Own Song with Three-String Chords

Here's your chance to write your first song. Follow these steps.

1. Draw a treble clef at the beginning of each staff.

2. Draw a $\frac{4}{4}$ time signature next to the treble clef in the first measure.

3. Fill in the bar lines and draw a repeat sign at the end.

4. Draw quarter-note slashes and quarter rests. You can choose which beats have slashes and which have rests, but be sure there are exactly four beats in each measure.

5. Choose which chords you want by filling in the chord frame above each measure.

6. Make up your own lyrics and write them below each staff.

7. **Have fun** and play your song on your guitar.

The Staff

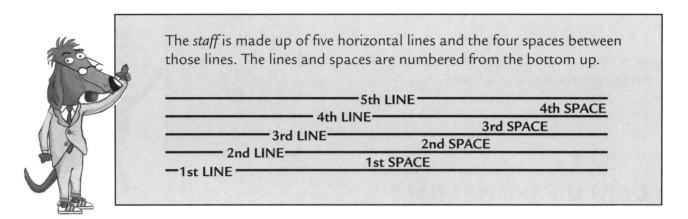

The *staff* is made up of five horizontal lines and the four spaces between those lines. The lines and spaces are numbered from the bottom up.

5th LINE
4th LINE — 4th SPACE
3rd LINE — 3rd SPACE
2nd LINE — 2nd SPACE
1st LINE — 1st SPACE

Name the line or space for each note.

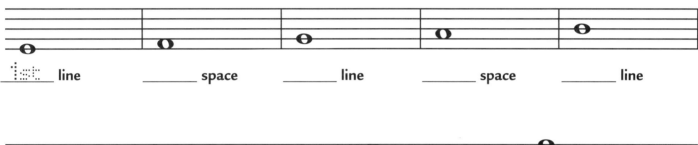

____1st____ line   _____ space   _____ line   _____ space   _____ line

_____ space   _____ line   _____ space   _____ line

Name the line for each note in the box below the staff.

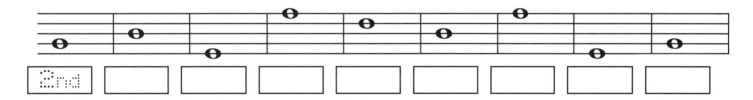

2nd								

Name the space for each note in the box below the staff.

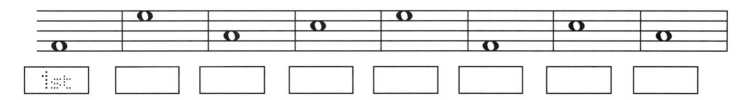

1st							

13

The Quarter Note

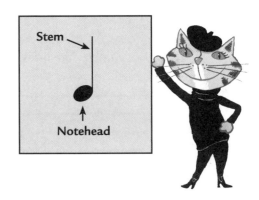

A *quarter note* has a black notehead and a stem.
Each quarter note equals one beat.

How to Draw the Quarter Note

Step 1:   To create the notehead, draw an oval and fill it in.
Draw several noteheads below in the third space.

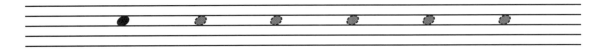

Step 2:   To create the stem, draw a line going down from
the left of the notehead to just below the staff.

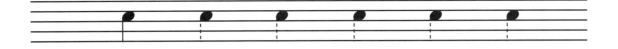

Now, draw six quarter notes on the third space of the staff.

Now, draw six quarter notes in the second space with
the stem going up from the right of the notehead.

Counting Time

Draw four quarter notes in each measure. In the first two measures, draw quarter notes having stems down,
and in the second two measures, draw quarter notes having stems up. Then, write the counts below the staff.

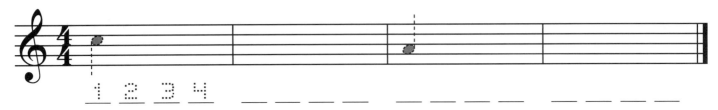

The Note E (1st String)

The note on the top space of the staff is called E.

Drawing the Note E

Step 1: Draw an oval notehead in the top space of the staff.

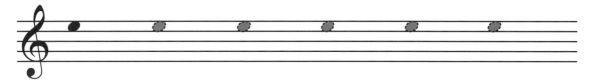

Step 2: For the stem, draw a line from the left of the notehead to the bottom space of the staff. The stem always goes down for this note.

Now, draw the note E six times below.

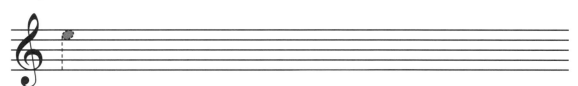

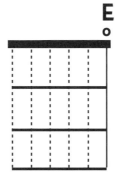

Playing the Note E

To play the note E, pick the open 1st string.

Indicate the fingering for note E by placing "**o**" above the 1st string on each diagram.

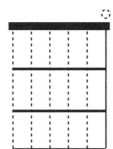
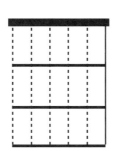
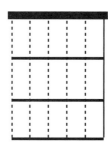

15

The Note F (1st String)

The note on the top line of the staff is called F.

Drawing the Note F

Drawing the note F is similar to drawing the note E, except the notehead is on the top line. On the staff below, draw the note F six times.

Playing the Note F

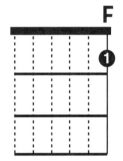

To play the note F, press the 1st string at the 1st fret.

On the diagram to the right, indicate the fingering for the note F by placing the number "1" in a circle on the 1st fret of the 1st string.

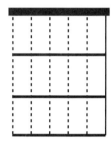

The Note G (1st String)

The note on the space above the staff is called G.

Drawing the Note G

To draw the note G on the staff, place the notehead on the space above the staff, and draw the stem down to the second line. On the staff below, draw the note G six times.

Playing the Note G

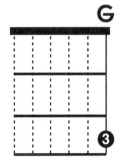

To play the note G, press the 1st string at the 3rd fret.

On the diagram to the right, indicate the fingering for the note G by placing the number "3" in a circle on the 3rd fret of the 1st string.

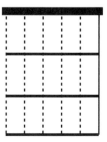

The Note B (2nd String)

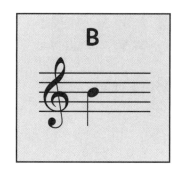

The note on the third line of the staff is called B.

Drawing the Note B

To draw the note B on the staff, place the notehead on the third line, and draw the stem down to just below the staff. On the staff below, draw the note B six times.

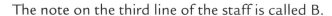

Playing the Note B

To play the note B, press the open 2nd string.

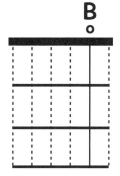

On the diagram to the right, indicate the fingering for the note B by placing "**o**" above the 2nd string.

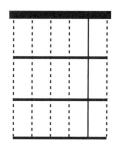

The Note C (2nd String)

The note on the third space of the staff is called C.

Drawing the Note C

To draw the note C on the staff, place the notehead on the third space, and draw the stem down to just below the staff. On the staff below, draw the note C six times.

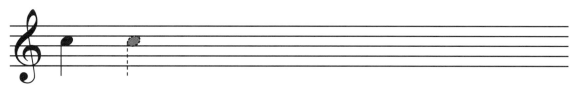

Playing the Note C

To play the note C, press the 2nd string at the 1st fret.

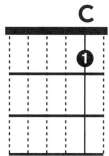

On the diagram to the right, indicate the fingering for the note C by placing the number "1" in a circle on the 1st fret of the 2nd string.

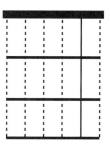

17

The Half Rest

A *half rest* means do not play for two beats.

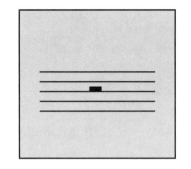

How to Draw the Half Rest

Step 1: Draw a box on top of the middle line of the staff.

Step 2: Fill in the box.

Now, draw six half rests.

The Note D (2nd String)

The note on the fourth line of the staff is called D.

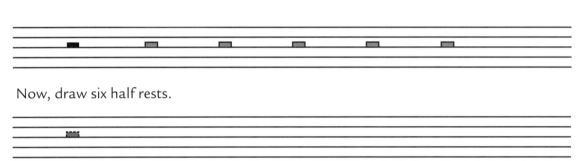

Drawing the Note D

To draw the note D on the staff, place the notehead on the fourth line, and draw the stem down to just below the staff. On the staff below, draw the note D six times.

Playing the Note D

To play the note D, press the 2nd string at the 3rd fret.

On the diagram to the right, indicate the fingering for the note D by placing the number "3" in a circle on the 3rd fret of the 2nd string.

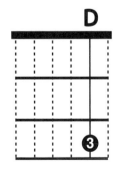

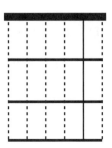

18

The Notes B, C, D, E, F, and G

B   C   D   E   F   G

Reading the Notes B, C, D, E, F, and G

Write the letter name of each note in the box below the staff.

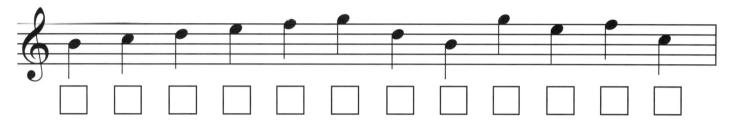

Word Fun with Notes

Write the letter name of each note on the line below
the staff. The notes in each measure spell a word!

Drawing the Notes B, C, D, E, F, and G

Write the noteheads first, and then add the stems going down.

Now, write all six notes in order from B to G two times.

19

Notes on the Strings: B, C, D, E, F, and G

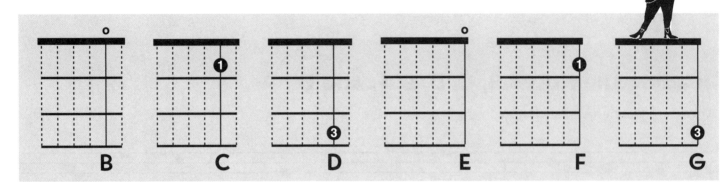

Write the correct note name below each fingered string.

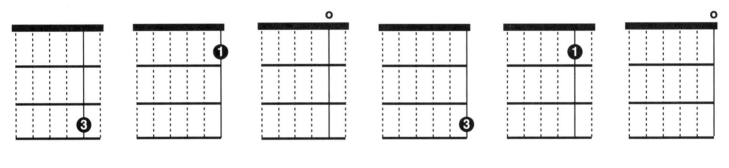

Draw the note on the staff above each note name. Use quarter notes.

C   E   G   B   D   F

Draw the fingering on the fretboard diagram above each note.

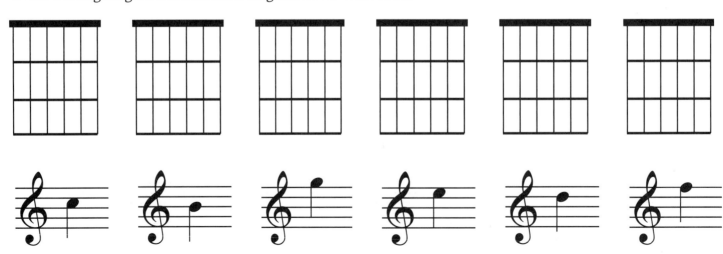

The Half Note

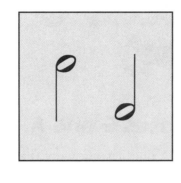

A *half note* lasts two beats. It is twice as long as a quarter note.

How to Draw the Half Note

Step 1: Create the notehead by drawing an oval. On the staff below, draw three noteheads in the third space and three noteheads in the second space.

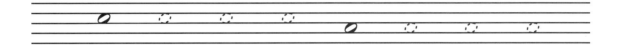

Step 2: Create the stems. For the first three notes, draw the stem going down from the left of the notehead, and for the second three notes, draw the stem going up from the right of the notehead.

Now, draw six half notes. Draw three on the third space, and three on the second space.

Counting Time

Fill in the missing beats by adding either a half rest or a half note in each measure.
Then, write the counts below the staff. Put parentheses around beats that are for rests.

The Notes G and A (3rd String)

Drawing the Notes G and A

To draw the notes G and A on the staff, write the noteheads first, and then add the stems going up.

Now, draw G and A on the staff once as quarter notes, then as half notes.

Quarter Notes   **Half Notes**

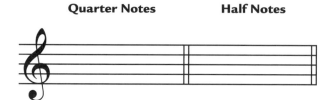

Playing the Note G

To play the note G, pick the open 3rd string.

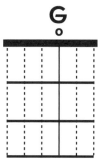

On the diagram to the right, indicate the fingering for the note G by placing "**o**" above the 3rd string.

Playing the Note A

To play the note A, press the 3rd string at the 2nd fret.

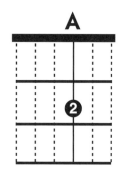

On the diagram to the right, indicate the fingering for the note A by placing the number "2" in a circle on the 2nd fret of the 3rd string.

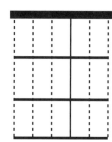

The Whole Note

A *whole note* lasts four beats.

How to Draw the Whole Note

Draw an oval in a space or on a line.

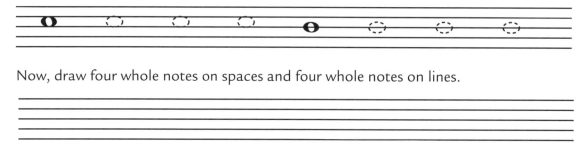

Now, draw four whole notes on spaces and four whole notes on lines.

Review: All the Notes and Chords in Book 1

Write the letter name of each note in the box below the staff.

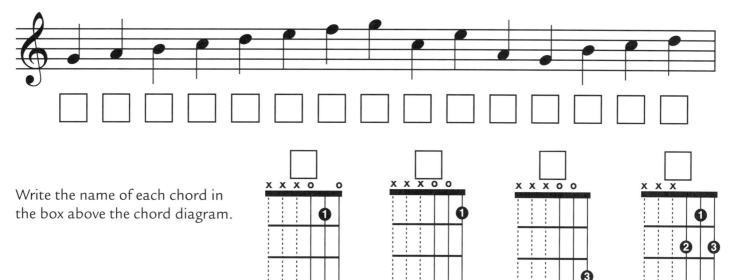

Write the name of each chord in the box above the chord diagram.

The Note D (4th String)

The note on the space below the staff is called D.

Drawing the Note D

To draw the note D on the staff, place the notehead on the space below the staff, and draw the stem up to the fourth line. On the staff below, draw the note D six times.

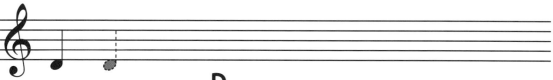

Playing the Note D

To play the note D, pick the open 4th string.

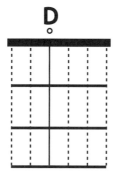

On the diagram to the right, indicate the fingering for the note D by placing "**o**" above the 4th string.

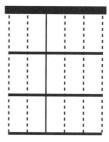

23

The Half-Note Slash

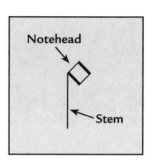

The *half-note slash* has a diamond-shaped notehead and a stem.
Each half-note slash lasts two beats, which is the same length as a half note.

How to Draw the Half-Note Slash

Step 1: Create the bottom half of the diamond-shaped notehead
by drawing a "v" from the middle line to the second line.

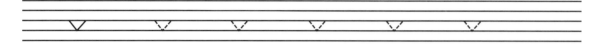

Step 2: Create the top half of the notehead by drawing an
upside-down "v" from the middle line to the fourth line.

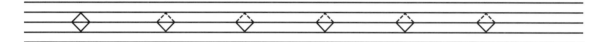

Step 3: Create the stem by drawing a line down from
the left of the notehead to just below the staff.

Now, draw six half-note slashes.

Counting Time

Fill in the missing beats with half-note slashes, and then write the counts below the staff.

___ ___   ___ ___   ___ ___   ___ ___   ___ ___

The Four-String G and G7 Chords

The Four-String G Chord

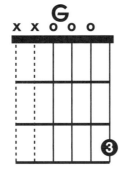

Draw the missing **x**'s and **o**'s for this four-string G chord.

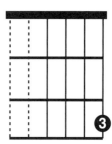

The Four-String G7 Chord

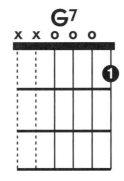

Draw the missing **x**'s and **o**'s for this four-string G7 chord.

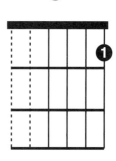

The Note E (4th String)

The note on the bottom line of the staff is called E.

Drawing the Note E

To draw the note E on the staff, place the notehead on the bottom line, and draw the stem up to just above the fourth line. On the staff below, draw the note E six times.

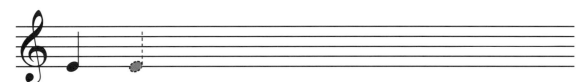

Playing the Note E

To play the note E, press the 4th string at the 2nd fret.

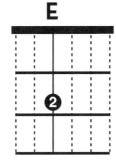

On the diagram to the right, indicate the fingering for the note E by placing the number "2" in a circle on the 2nd fret of the 4th string.

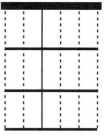

25

The Four-String C Chord

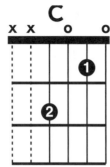

Draw the missing **x**'s and **o**'s for this four-string C chord.

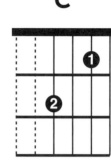

Write Your Own Song with Four-String Chords

Here is your chance to write a song with four-string chords. Follow these steps.

1. Draw a treble clef at the beginning of each staff.

2. Draw a $\frac{4}{4}$ time signature next to the treble clef in the first measure.

3. Fill in the bar lines and draw a repeat sign at the end.

4. Draw quarter-note slashes, half-note slashes, quarter rests, and half rests. You can choose which beats have slashes and which have rests, but be sure there are exactly four beats in each measure.

5. Choose the four-string chords you want to use (G, G⁷, or C) by filling in the chord frame above each measure.

6. Make up your own lyrics and write them below each staff.

7. **Have fun** and play your song on your guitar.

Common Time

This symbol **C** is a time signature that means the same as $\frac{4}{4}$ time. There are four beats to each measure.

How to Draw the Common Time Signature

Draw a letter "C" from the fourth line to the second line.

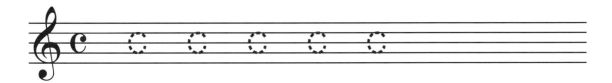

Now, draw six common time signatures.

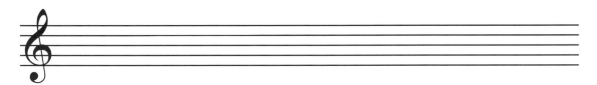

The Note F (4th String)

F

The note on the bottom space of the staff is called F.

Drawing the Note F

To draw the note F on the staff, place the notehead in the bottom space, and draw the stem up to the top line. On the staff below, draw the note F six times.

Playing the Note F

To play the note F, press the 4th string at the 3rd fret.

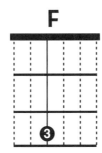

F

On the diagram to the right, indicate the fingering for the note F by placing the number "3" in a circle on the 3rd fret of the 4th string.

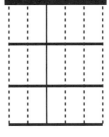

27

Notes on the Strings: D, E, F, G, and A

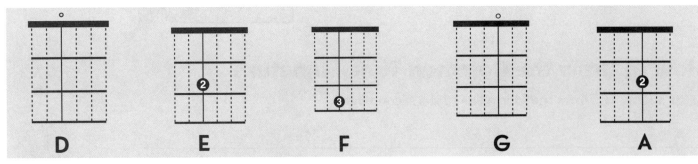

D   E   F   G   A

Write the note names below the fingered strings.

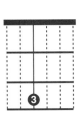  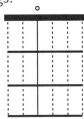 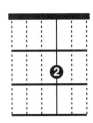 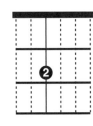

___   ___   ___   ___   ___

Draw each note on the staff above the note name. Use whole notes.

E   G   D   F   A

Draw the fingering on the fretboard diagram above each note.

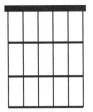  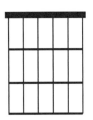  

Write Your Own Melody with the Notes D, E, F, G, and A

Compose a short melody with the notes D, E, F, G, and A. Use quarter notes, half notes, and whole notes. Remember that only four beats fit in each measure.

The Dotted Half Note

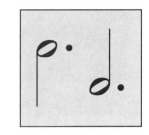

The *dotted half note* lasts three beats.

How to Draw the Dotted Half Note

Step 1: Draw a half note.

Step 2: Add a dot to the right of the notehead.

Now, draw three dotted half notes with stems going up and three dotted half notes with stems going down.

The 3/4 Time Signature

A 3/4 time signature means there are three equal beats in every measure.

How to Draw the 3/4 Time Signature

Step 1: Draw a number "3" sitting on top of the third line of the staff.

Step 2: Draw a number "4" sitting on the bottom line below the number 3.

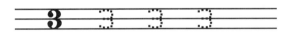 

Now, draw six 3/4 time signatures.

Choose the Time Signature

Each of the following examples has either three or four beats in each measure. Place either 4/4, C, or 3/4 at the beginning of each example. Use each time signature only once.

Time Signature

Time Signature

Time Signature

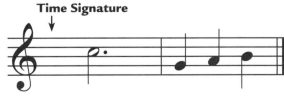

The Notes A, B, and C (5th String)

The notes A, B, and C all use *ledger lines*. Ledger lines extend the staff up or down.

Drawing the Note A

Step 1: Draw two short ledger lines below the staff.

Step 2: Draw a notehead on the lowest ledger line.

Step 3: Add a stem going up from the right of the notehead.

Playing the Note A

To play the note A, pick the open 5th string.

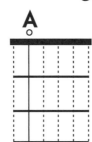

On the diagram to the right, indicate the fingering for the note A by placing "**o**" above the 5th string.

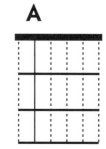

Drawing the Notes B and C

B and C are written the same as A, but B is written on the space below just one ledger line.

C is written on the ledger line just below the staff.

Playing the Note B

To play the note B, press the 5th string at the 2nd fret.

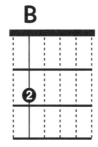

On the diagram to the right, indicate the fingering for the note B by placing the number "2" in a circle on the 2nd fret of the 5th string.

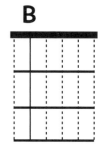

Playing the Note C

To play the note C, press the 5th string at the 3rd fret.

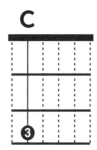

On the diagram to the right, indicate the fingering for the note C by placing the number "3" in a circle on the 3rd fret of the 5th string.

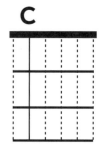

Draw the notes A, B, C once as quarter notes, once as half notes, and once as whole notes.

Quarter Notes

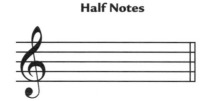

Half Notes

Whole Notes

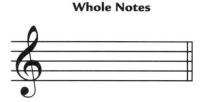

The Dotted-Half-Note Slash

The *dotted-half-note slash* lasts three beats, the same length as the dotted half note.

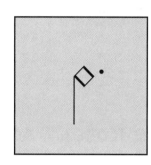

How to Draw the Dotted-Half-Note Slash

Step 1: Draw a half-note slash.

Step 2: Add a dot to the right of the notehead.

Now, draw six dotted-half-note slashes.

Write the Number of Beats

Here are all the types of notes, slashes, and rests you know so far. Write the number of beats each symbol receives (1, 2, 3, or 4) on the line below the staff.

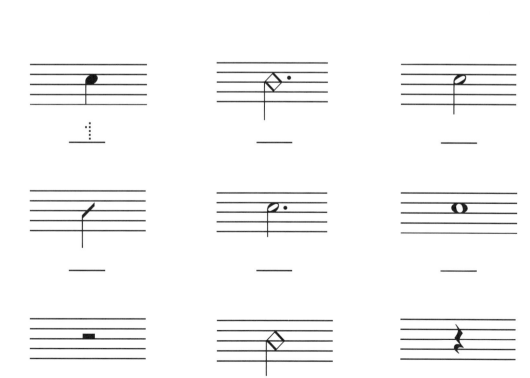

The Notes E and F (6th String)

Drawing the Notes E and F

The notes E and F both use ledger lines. Draw the ledger lines first, then the noteheads, and finish up by drawing the stems going up.

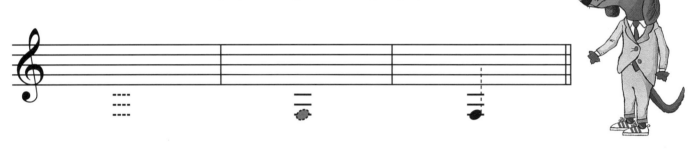

Now, draw E and F on the staff once as quarter notes, once as half notes, and once as whole notes.

Quarter Notes	Half Notes	Whole Notes
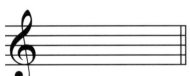		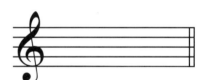

Playing the Note E

To play the note E, pick the open 6th string.

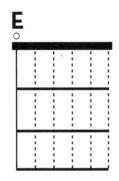

On the diagram to the right, indicate the fingering for the note E by placing "**o**" above the 6th string.

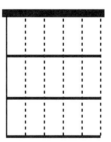

Playing the Note F

To play the note F, press the 6th string at the 1st fret.

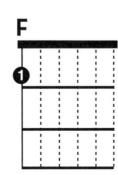

On the diagram to the right, indicate the fingering for the note F by placing the number "1" in a circle on the 1st fret of the 6th string.

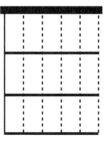

The Fermata

A *fermata* means to play the note a little longer than normal (usually about twice the normal length). The fermata is sometimes called a "bird's eye."

How to Draw the Fermata

Step 1: Draw the top half of a circle above the note.

Step 2: Place a dot inside the half circle.

Now, draw a fermata over each of the notes below.

33

Book 2, page 28

The Note G (6th String)

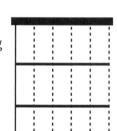

The note on the space two ledger lines below the staff is called G.

Drawing the Note G

To draw the note G on the staff, first draw two ledger lines below the staff. Then, place the notehead in the space below the second ledger line and draw the stem up to the third line. On the staff to the right, draw the note G six times.

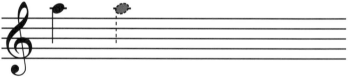

Playing the Note G

To play the note G, press the 6th string at the 3rd fret.

On the diagram to the right, indicate the fingering for the note G by placing the number "3" in a circle on the 3rd fret of the 6th string.

Book 2, page 32

The Note High A (1st String)

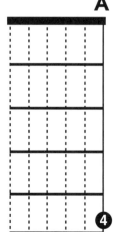

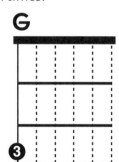

The note one ledger line above the staff is called high A.

Drawing the Note High A

To draw the note high A on the staff, first draw one ledger line above the staff. Then, place the notehead on the ledger line and draw the stem down to the third line. On the staff to the right, draw the note high A six times.

Playing the Note High A

To play the note high A, press the 1st string at the 5th fret.

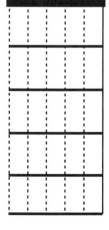

On the diagram to the right, indicate the fingering for the note high A by placing the number "4" in a circle on the 5th fret of the 1st string.

Notes on the Strings: E, F, G, A, B, C, and High A

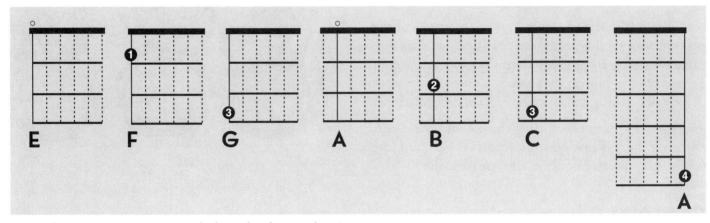

Write the correct note names below the fingered strings.

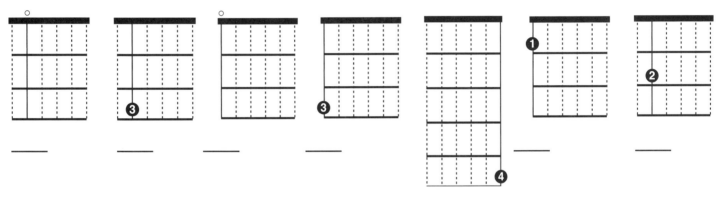

Draw the note on the staff above each note name. Use dotted half notes.

F   A   C   High A   E   G   B

Draw the fingering on the fretboard diagram above each note.

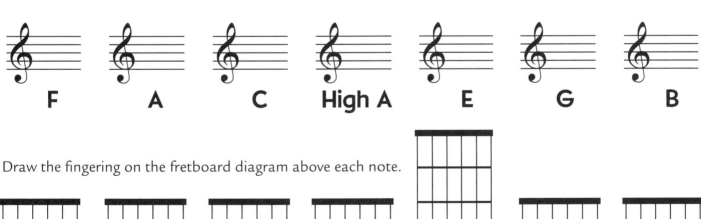

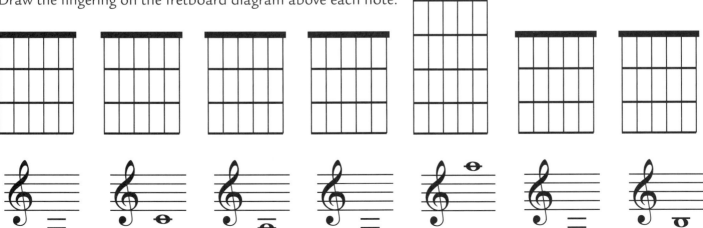

Pickup Measures

Not all pieces of music begin on the first beat of a measure. Sometimes music begins with just part of a measure, which is called a *pickup*.

A pickup is like a pumpkin pie. If you were to cut the pie into four equal pieces and take one piece away, there would be three pieces left. If you are playing in $\frac{4}{4}$ time and the pickup measure has one quarter note, there will be three quarter notes in the last measure.

Playing in $\frac{3}{4}$ time is like cutting the pie into three equal pieces: if there is one quarter note as the pickup, there will be two quarter notes in the last measure.

Counting Time

For each example, write the counts for the pickup measure and the final measure under the staff. Put parentheses around the counts that aren't played.

Tempo Signs

A *tempo sign* tells you how fast to play the music. Below are the three most common tempo signs.

Andante means to play **slow.**

Moderato means to play **moderately.**

Allegro means to play **fast.**

Writing Tempo Signs

Write the correct tempo sign next to the speed that matches.

slow _____ **moderately** _____ **fast** _____

Three-String Chords as Notes

Three-String C Chord

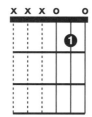

Here is the chord shown as notes.

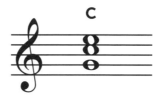

Write the three-string C chord as notes on the staff.

Three-String G Chord

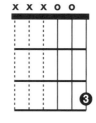

Here is the chord shown as notes.

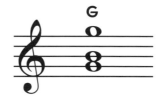

Write the three-string G chord as notes on the staff.

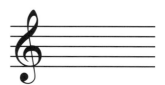

Three-String G⁷ Chord

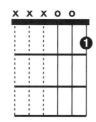

Here is the chord shown as notes.

Write the three-string G⁷ chord as notes on the staff.

Write three-note chords as notes on the staff below the chord names. Use quarter notes and half notes. Remember to use only four beats per measure because of the $\frac{4}{4}$ time signature.

37

Four-String Chords as Notes

Four-String C Chord

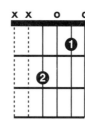

Here is the chord shown as notes.

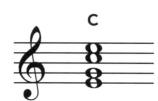

Write the four-string C chord as notes on the staff.

Four-String G Chord

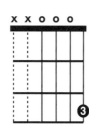

Here is the chord shown as notes.

Write the four-string G chord as notes on the staff.

Four-String G⁷ Chord

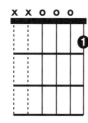

Here is the chord shown as notes.

Write the four-string G^7 chord as notes on the staff.

Write four-note chords as notes on the staff below the chord names. Use quarter notes, half notes, and dotted half notes. Remember to use only three beats per measure because of the $\frac{3}{4}$ time signature.

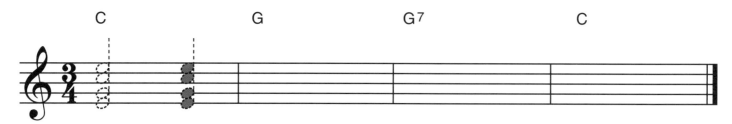

Dynamics

Writing Dynamics

Dynamics are symbols that tell you how loud or soft to play. Below are the four most common dynamics.

Write the correct dynamic sign next to its definition.

p stands for *piano*, which means **soft**.

mf stands for *mezzo-forte*, which means **moderately loud**.

f stands for *forte*, which means **loud**.

ff stands for *fortissimo*, which means **very loud.**

loud _____

soft _____

very loud _____

moderately loud _____

38

The Whole Rest

A *whole rest* means do not play for a whole measure.

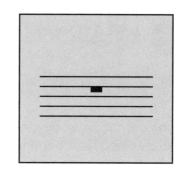

How to Draw the Whole Rest

Step 1: Draw a box under the bottom of the middle line of the staff.

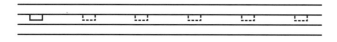

Now, draw six whole rests.

Step 2: Fill in the box.

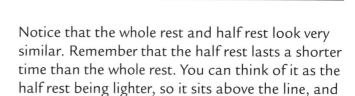

Notice that the whole rest and half rest look very similar. Remember that the half rest lasts a shorter time than the whole rest. You can think of it as the half rest being lighter, so it sits above the line, and the whole rest is heavier, so it falls below the line.

Ties

A *tie* is a curved line that connects two of the same note. When two notes are tied, don't play the second note, but add the two notes together instead.

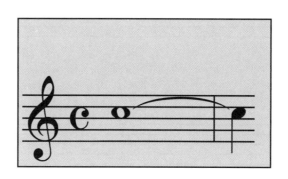

How to Draw the Tie

When the notes being tied are on or above the middle line of the staff, the curve of the tie goes up.

When the notes being tied are below the middle line of the staff, the curve of the tie goes down.

Draw ties to connect the notes below. Then write the total number of beats for each pair on the line below the staff.

5 beats

_____

_____

_____

_____

_____

Writing Music Using Everything You've Learned So Far

It is now time for you to compose your own music! Make sure to include a treble clef, time signature, tempo sign, bar lines, all kinds of notes and rests, three-note chords and four-note chords, dynamics, and ties. If you like, you may also include fermatas, pickup measures, and lyrics. Be creative and write music you'd like to play for your friends, parents, or teachers.

If you want to write more music, purchase blank manuscript paper such as Alfred's Basic Music Writing Book (item 6700) and keep learning as you write.